"Thinking I Hear Thee Call"

FRANCES M LYNCH and PATRICIA FARA

CHERYL FRANCES-HOAD

14
S.
El.
mp
work at Mar - co - ni's New Street Wind - ing ___ shop ma - king ra - di - o
00:33
A
16
sets. I've been 'ere since just af - ter
00:39
18
World War One and stayed all through World War Two.
00:44
20
mf
I got this let - ter from the King, and this Bri - tish Em - pire
00:49

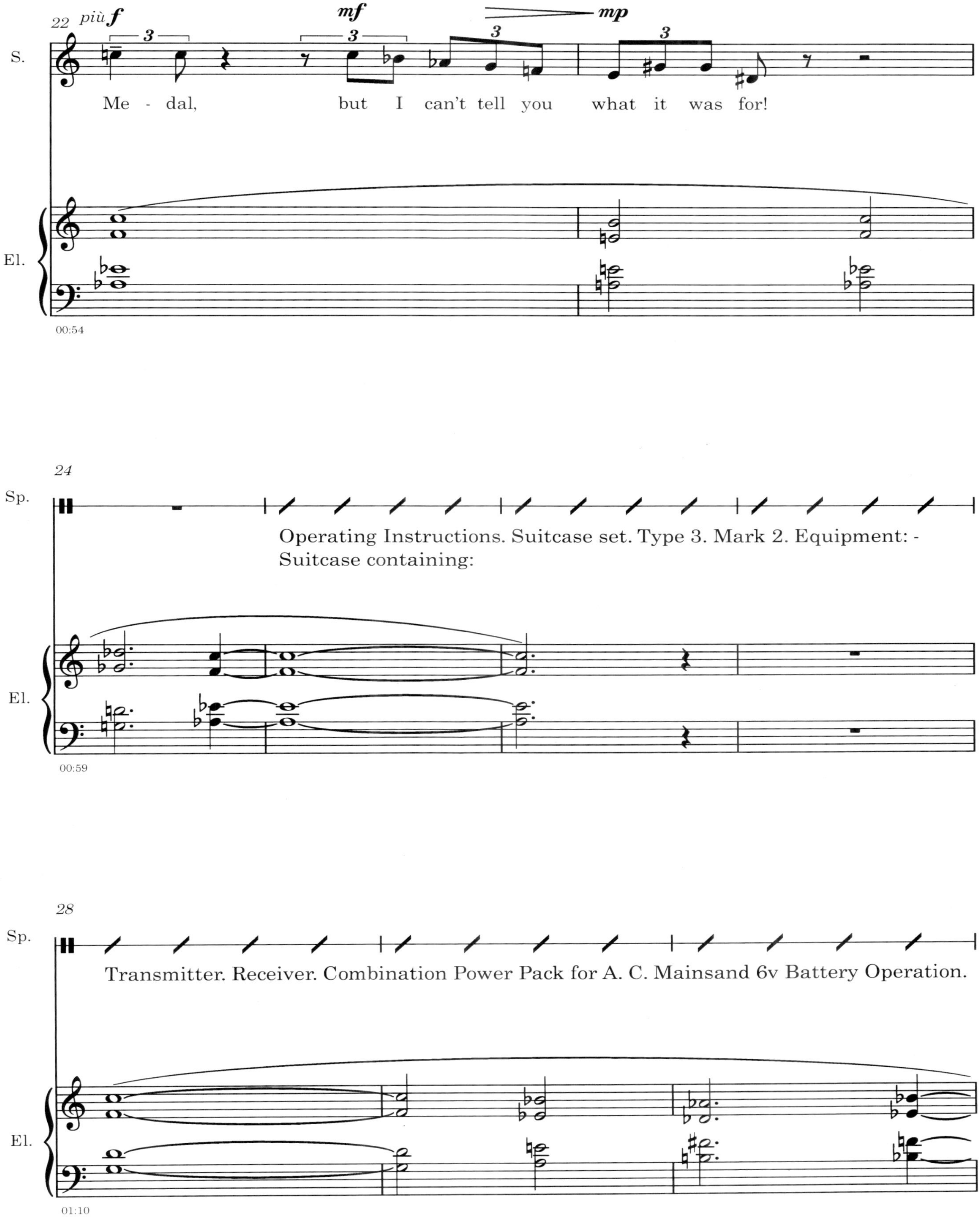
22
più f
mf
mp
S.
Me - dal, but I can't tell you what it was for!
El.
00:54
24
Sp.
Operating Instructions. Suitcase set. Type 3. Mark 2. Equipment: -
Suitcase containing:
El.
00:59
28
Sp.
Transmitter. Receiver. Combination Power Pack for A. C. Mainsand 6v Battery Operation.
El.
01:10

B
31
mf
You can't get more Es - sex than me, I was
S.
Sp.
Instruction manual.
El.
01:18
33
p
born in Chelms - ford, been 'ere all my life. I start - ed
01:23
35
mp
poco
off on the shop floor work - ing on one of the long rows of
Spares Box containing: 100 ft aerial wire.
01:28

38
poco
S.
5
3
bench - es with four or five of us girls on one side.
Sp.
10ft earth wire.
Transmitting Key.
El.
01:36
41
Sp.
Telephone headset. 10 fuses (two types)
1 Receiving value 7Q7.
El.
01:44
44
C
mp
S.
3
3
The on - ly man in the room the su - per - vi - sor
El.
01:52

46
mf
mp
S.
was walk - ing a - round ma - king sure we had our heads down, so we kept
El.
01:57
48
S.
bu - sy do - ing the same fi - ni - cky
Sp.
1 Receiving valve 7R7.
El.
02:02
50
mf
S.
tasks, day af - ter day,
Sp.
1 Transmitting value EL 32.
1 Transmitting Valve 6L6G. Screwdriver. Two brass pins to convert...
El.
02:07

53
S.
day af - ter day
Sp.
...mains plug to Continental fittings. 4 tank coils. 4 Crystals.
Total Weight: 34 lbs.
El.
02:15
56
D
mp
un - til our backs ached
and our fin - gers were
02:23
58
sore.
Before setting up to establish communication, the proposed site should be examined as to its suitability for the...
02:28

61
Sp.
...installation of an efficient Aerial and Earth system, and the question of a power supply considered. If mains are not available, a 6-volt accumulator may be procured...
El.
02:36
68
Sp.
... this should be of the automobile type, fully charged and in good condition. Two such batteries may, with advantage, be used in parallel.
Open the suitcase, and examine the apparatus.
Morse sounds
El.
02:54
E
74
mf cantabile
poco
S.
Du - ring World War Two I worked in a small room,
mf
El.
03:10

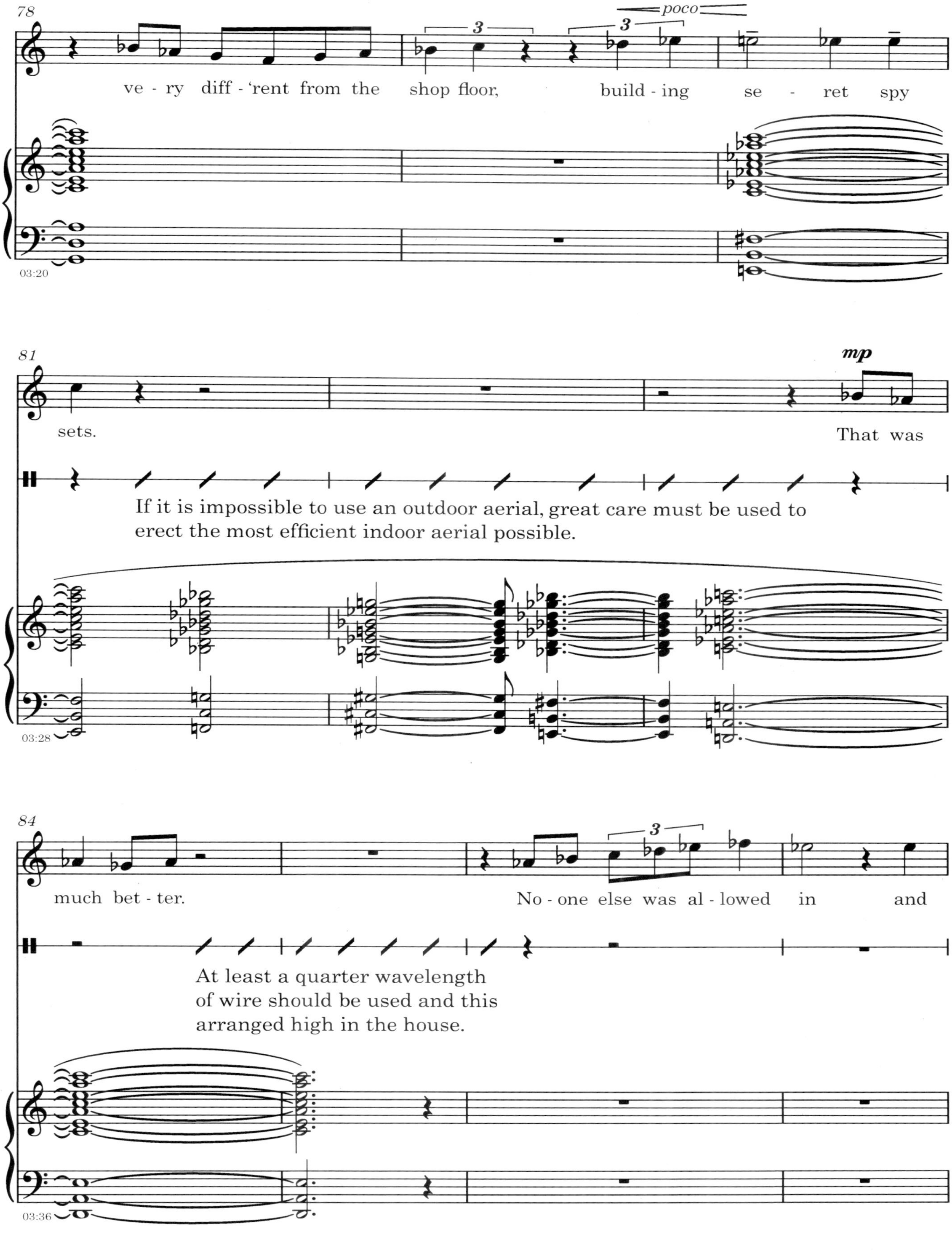
78
poco
S.
ve - ry diff - 'rent from the shop floor, build - ing se - ret spy
El.
03:20
81
mp
S.
sets. That was
Sp.
If it is impossible to use an outdoor aerial, great care must be used to erect the most efficient indoor aerial possible.
El.
03:28
84
S.
much bet - ter. No - one else was al - lowed in and
Sp.
At least a quarter wavelength of wire should be used and this arranged high in the house.
El.
03:36

88
mf
f
3
S.
I was the su - per - vi - sor, so there were no
El.
03:46
91
mp
F
men, no men at all. We knew we were in -
03:54
94
- volved in some - thing ve - ry im - por - tant and se - cret,
04:02

99
S.
so we all had a
Sp.
Should circumstances restrict activities to one room, the aerial wire should be arranged in zig-zag fashion across the room about a foot below the ceiling.
El.
04:15
104
G
f
mp
great sense of pride,
and ne - ver breathed a word
04:28
109
of what we did out - side—
mp
04:41

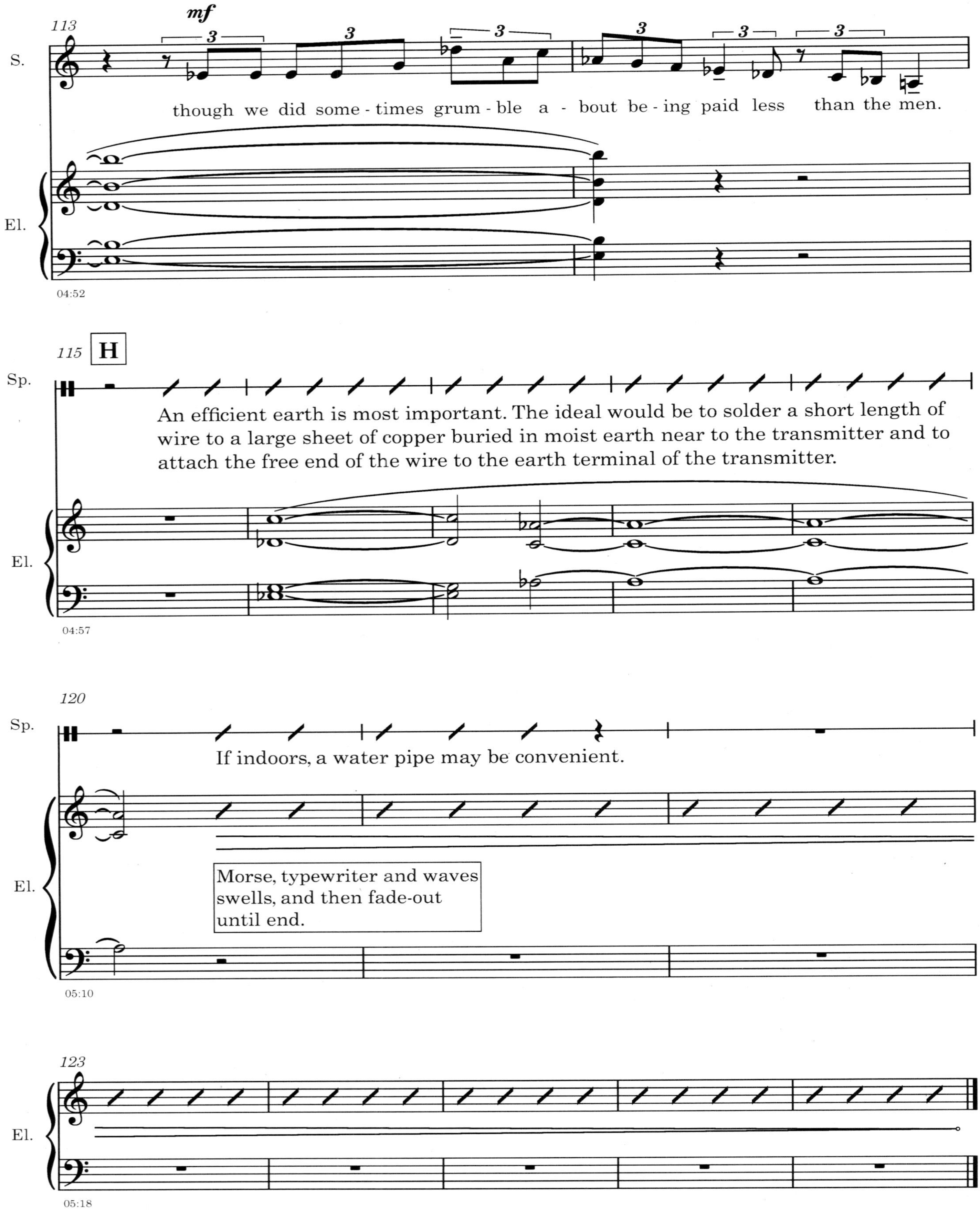
113
mf
S.
though we did some - times grum - ble a - bout be - ing paid less than the men.
El.
04:52
115
H
Sp.
An efficient earth is most important. The ideal would be to solder a short length of wire to a large sheet of copper buried in moist earth near to the transmitter and to attach the free end of the wire to the earth terminal of the transmitter.
El.
04:57
120
Sp.
If indoors, a water pipe may be convenient.
El.
Morse, typewriter and waves swells, and then fade-out until end.
05:10
123
El.
05:18